A POETIC BREAK THROUGH

SABRINA BASHAM

A POETIC BREAK THROUGH

Sabrina Basham
A Poetic Break Through
All rights reserved.
Copyright © 2024 by Sabrina Basham

Published by Spines
ISBN: 979-8-89383-736-0

CONTENTS

CHAPTER 1
CAUGHT IN A STORM

She suddenly awakens from sleep
Sometimes in the dead of night
Due to a nightmare that gave her a fright
She's drenched in her own sweat
But she's trying to catch her breath
Still trying her hardest to avoid
So many vivid thoughts she has of death
She began staring out her window
Watching the color of the sky change
From blue, purple, orange and black
Which seemed to her really kind of strange
Big fat raindrops begin to fall quickly
From the dark and gloomy sky
Then she suddenly developed a feeling in her gut
With pain so intense she wanted more than to cry
Lightning strikes loudly and the wind begins to pick up
more speed
With rotation getting faster and faster
Gaining more power and hunger to feed
Destroying everything within its path
Leaving nothing behind but a very huge aftermath
Time passed fast while the tornado constantly grew
and grew
Rotating into a funnel cloud getting closer and closer to
her home
Like a thief in the night
Taking all she had ever known
Quickly flying from the window she stood by
Thinking about where she would plan to hide
Then into her closet, she ran in like a flash
Sitting on the floor with her dog by her side.

CHAPTER 2
CAUGHT IN TIME

I'm caught up in time
My clock suddenly stops
My heart skips a beat
My stomach flips and flops
Chills run up my back then down my legs
A sudden pain soon turns into fiery heat
Hard to breathe which creates a sudden sweat
Across my neck and beneath my feet
No doctor could ever diagnose or find
My own sickness actually created
Only within my very own mind
It's a simple answer and easy to find
Just embracing each and every moment
While I'm caught within the time
No cure, no treatment.
I'm overfilled with defeatment
Only destiny's rhyme can bring back my sanity
That's guaranteed to be taken with time
But dare do I dream my time is taken back
For the key to knowledge is just what I lack
Stuck within my very own mind
Left with no reason why I'm caught in time

CHAPTER 3
FALLEN ANGEL

She wakes up from a deep sleep
Found completely twisted in chains
She's unable to move
Because of her fierce pain
Her head is throbbing.
Feeling as though she's been hit by a train
She loses oxygen, turning blue
As she slowly drowns at sea
Praying a miracle will soon set her free
The sunlight reflects into the ocean
Revealing her beaten and broken face
Her body slowly sinks down to the ocean floor
Where not a soul could ever be traced.
All she used was self-defense
Fighting intruders with her knife
Never considering the consequences of her actions
Or ever even losing her life
Looking through the water
Visualizing dark shadows in the sky
They share her down yet laugh at her struggles
No one will help her, but watch her die
She reflects on her life and her memories
As she asked God why me?
Shadows quickly fade in and out
She has visions that no one will cry
Suddenly an angel appears in her sight
Reaching out with both hands to her
He told her everything would be all right
Then she grasped his hand.
He gently pulls her out of the water

Her fragile body lay broken there in the sand
Then he heals her damaged body
And it physically takes away all her pain
Then he cleansed her soul completely
Leaving her smiling and mentally sane
He decided to make her an angel.
She begins growing beautiful white wings
Then God called her home to heaven
Where she begins to rejoice and to sing
She stands her ground at the Golden Gate
She's grinning beautifully from ear to ear
She has no feelings of hate or revenge
She no longer has feelings of fear
But the angel that saved her gave up his power
He stayed trapped for eternity on earth
Giving up his wings to her
Knowing exactly what she was worth
He completed his assignment
Doing exactly what God had asked
His job now on earth was to unmask
All the ones are dark and masked

CHAPTER 4
GOD WHY ME?

God why me
Send me a sign
To set me free
Help me survive
Throughout the day
Give me the strength
To live the right way
Walk with me, God.
Through the field of lies
Please grant me courage.
To cut off all my bad tithes
Give me warmth
On those cold
And lonely nights
Ward away these demons
So I can avoid having to fight
God why me?
Please answer me why?
I want to know the reasons
You didn't let me die
Please grant me sanity.
To live for tomorrow
To avoid my depression
All this hate and sorrow
God just so you know
I've done nothing but good
I'm constantly helping others
Doing what I think I should
Please make me an angel
So I can deal with the ones who hate

It may seem quite ironic
But I believe it's my fate
God why me
I ask you again and again
Show me a sign or a miracle
Create me as my very own true friend
Grant me a charm
Just a piece of good luck
Just to increase my chances
A guarantee to keep me safe from harm
Please give me the energy
To continue making a difference
Always putting others first
And observing continuously
While gaining more experience
Showing my love and care
No matter how thick or thin
One more question dear God.
When will my life begin?
God why me?

CHAPTER 5
HALLOWEEN

Tonight is the night of Halloween
A celebration of the dead
One night is guaranteed.
A conversation to be left unsaid
When things don't go right
And the moon is so big and bright
Chills run up and down my spine
Leaving awkward thoughts within my mind
Goosebumps suddenly begin to appear
Just a sign that something is near
Tonight is the night of Halloween
When ghosts and goblins
Can cause a scene
Demons come out to give you a scare
Trick or treat, do you dare?
Wolves all around me howling
Monsters stalk me with their prowling
Their teeth are all shiny and razor sharp
Out in the dark, a bite in their bark
Guaranteed to make you scream
Only this is the night of hallows eve
Tonight is the night of Halloween
When the paranormal becomes a true reality
Trick or treaters end their night
Then the weirdos came out
In the dark and play
Killer clowns come and look for a fight
An unexpected comedy
And the amusement begins
Till the lights come back on

The lost souls to hell resend
The night passed so quick
The kids ate too much candy
And they made themselves sick
Next year I bet they
Will be sure to think twice
To trick or treat
Either way you'll pay a price
Tonight is the night of Halloween
It's been an adventure
Almost like a bad dream
So glad to spend one night out free
Having fun and laughing with friends
Not alone or by myself
All tied to a tree.

CHAPTER 6
I LOVE YOU

I love you more with each passing day
I love you to the moon and back
I love you to the stars
I love you more than the galaxy itself
And all the way past the planet Mars
I love you deeper than the ocean and sea
I know this because all the things that mattered before
Now don't matter at all to me
I love you like a fat kid loves cake, candy or soda pop
I will love you till the end of time
When everything suddenly comes to a stop
I love you more than my acoustic guitar
And that my dear, explains my love a lot
I even love you more than alcohol
Which really hits the spot
I love you more than any drug
Because you are the medicine that saved my life
So glad to be your everything and your wife
I love you more than any other soul
For you were the one who helped me out of the hole
So it's you that I choose to forever grow old
I love you more than the number of books I've ever read
And more than the place where I rest my head
I love you more than my most happiest memory
Or my greatest idealistic invention yet
I love you more than my biggest and greatest dreams
And if you don't believe me we can make a bet
I know that I love you and my mind is set

CHAPTER 7

IT'S THE HOLIDAY SEASON

It's the holiday season
So it's the holiday season
I'm completely in a daze
Without a single clue or reason
Left sitting within silence
No words can I say
I keep hitting failure all the time
Regardless of the time of day
I'm just trying to make it
Without having to fake it
No way of grasping control of my life
So here I am on my knees
Now to God I beg and pray "oh please!"
It's the holiday season
Not yet have I bought a single gift
Everything I once owned
Now forever gone due to being stole
No other choice but to survive and shoplift
I'm left hungry and homeless
No car can I roll
With no warmth or a jacket
All alone without feeling or knowing love
My heart begins to slowly grow cold
No respect so I refuse to defend and protect
So outside here is where I sleep
Wrapped up in newspaper I will forever keep
In the park on a bench in the cold
Happy holiday season to you and to yours
I wish I had been more thankful

For all that I had
I would have made better choices
And with that my heart forever blood pours
It's the holiday season
Yet my mind continuously sores
With a solution, if considered
Will in fact forever be one taskful chore.

CHAPTER 8
A LIFE TOGETHER

One love, two hearts
Two free-floating souls
Forever together
Never to part.
Happy endings and some
New beginnings
Living life
True love
Constantly sending
Together content
Truly happy, without the needed consent
Another heart to be conceived
Now together as three
A new rhythm, can it be?
Two hearts beating as one
And now there are three
One happy little family
Working harder together
Because nothing in life comes free
A new start costs
Overnight packing
Moving far away overseas
Safe and sound
Let them stare, no care have we
Of being considered the perfect pair
Cause only a life together
This is where we
Are always known as
Happy you'll see.

LIFE WITHOUT LOVE

Feeling incomplete and empty inside
All around me are struggles and pain
Visual and physical love is truly undefined
Left with misery and hateful thoughts to unbind
Living and breathing life without love
Is a lonely dark and miserable life worth living?
But a gift of knowledge is assumed to not be defined as
A life worth living free as a dove
It's considered to be a realistic fate
To be alone, in love yet still waiting
Keeping calm as well as my steady heart rate
Where my story begins remains a question unknown
They must eventually end so I will no longer be alone
My depression sets in as I wait by the door
Patiently waiting for my love to come home

CHAPTER 10

LIFE IS WORTH LIVING

Our choices are made every day.
Help the world go round
Make one small slip
You will end up lost and drug-bound.
No way to learn
But to live and survive
In this life we know it is worth living
There's something everybody dies for
So secretive in fact
It's a life worth living
It's hard as hell to find myself still in tacked
Only interest of a specific kind
To keep what's left of my precious mind
Only drug found to help me rewind
Within minutes gone but careful or it's on
I hear the county blues are in town
And they run real big and steep
Watching us at every corner
So, we know exactly when it's getting deep
Making all that good money
Working hard as hell on our own two feet
Getting phone calls every day.
About whom to keep around
And who will bring the heat
Makes this life worth living
When I know it's safe and sound
Like a sudden pause in time
Unless your street mob living.
And you got the urge to rhyme
From inside a life worth living

And that's a choice truly undefined
Living free and on the edge
Only now within my own mind
Creates happiness inside my soul
No one is bound to find
Speeding up my heart rate
That is in fact so broken from all the hate
It's crazy but realistic
Visualization of my absolute fate
Completely content physically and emotionally
Happy living a life worth living for
Goodness sake, locked away
Into a reality unable to hide
With no way at all to hit rewind
When we talked to each other, we could confide
Ready to live a life worth living
Having high hopes, it is you by my side
With no more rules that we have to abide.

CHAPTER II
LONELINESS

Complete loneliness inside
On the outside I love undefined
To live a life without misery and hate
It is in fact no life at all but really of fate
Where my story begins is in question
Combined with what I fear is the end
An emptiness overflows and surrounds me with shadows
So depressed not a care given by friends
My history begins repeating itself. It all had me
exhausted so ready for some sleep
Just to feel someone's touch again we're making me
finally complete
Just one slow kiss with love
Make me feel my heart
They're in my last dying wish
Then I will swim free like a fish
Left behind without any sanity, I began to fake my smile
and I tried my hardest to hide my tears.
Self stuck in the moment of overcoming my fears
Nothing else to do but keep fighting
Here I am stuck within my mind
Any chance of living without him beside me
Nothing feels right. Everything goes dark
And finally I began losing my sight

CHAPTER 12

LOVE LETTER

To the man who truly holds my heart
The man who was there
For me from the very start
He gave me a home
And healed my fragile broken heart
He holds the tiny pieces
In both hands with care
Gluing each piece together with love
Mend slowly with each and every tear
He accepted me and my flaws
Always keeping me close in mind
Constantly showing me his love
Which I honestly think
That I would never find
He is my strength and power
When I am weak or extremely ill
The one man who always held me close
And showed me exactly what is real
From the beginning I did better alone
But after our first kiss I knew
In his arms I felt more like home
He is my rock.
Without him I'd be in jail
After reaching mental reality
I'm guaranteed to do nothing but fail
Here are my vows written for and only for you
With my feelings submitted to love so true
I promise to accept you for all that you are
I am yours forever and I will follow you
No matter how far

I promise to love you unconditionally
Communicate and stay 100% true
I will stand my ground beside you
With my full support in whatever it is
That you want to do.

CHAPTER 13
NOTE TO SELF

Dear self,
We need answers
Our bodies secretly hide
Its effects of cancer
Unable to confide in
Unable to share
Because no one acknowledges
No one else cares
As time flies by quickly
Proofs show your heartache
Mind unable to grasp
Your true meaning
Your overall purpose
Before life as you know it
God finally takes
Left behind is only
A simple note to self
Filled with only questions
But no answers are defined
What's wrong with your health
You try and you try
But fail to find your wealth
Only recognized for your madness
Your questions of what if
And why you are known now
By only reading your
Note's to self
Your body is dying
Yet you still fight for your fate

You could just give up
But instead you refuse
You grow tired of the consistent silence
Becoming sick of life's abuse
You get stuck for a reason.
Never giving up
Yet learn to accept your choices
Choosing what drugs to use
Just a note to self
To never lose or have
Any regrets that follow
Life's effects are from
Life's choices that you choose.

CHAPTER 14
ONE TIRED MOM

One tired mom finally gets some peace and quiet
Finally a chance to reflect and rewind
Trying to convince herself not to lose her mind
One tired mom who always keeps on going
She never stops for herself, even when her children
Have finally stopped growing
She always hides her pain, until late at night
And after everyone has been fed
Sound asleep and tucked into their beds
She let's her emotions out really slow
And that's when her tears like a river begin to flow
One tired mom unable to rest
With no one to remind her
Just how well she passes each and every test
Someone to tell her she was doing a great job
Being a mom who tries her best
One tired mom who forgets her self worth
After all her sacrifice just to give birth
To a child that will one day have no choice
But to live each day without ever again hearing her voice
They will be left with only precious memories
And her teachings of survival
How to simply be kind and show love
Even your worst enemies
One tired mom watches you sleep
Making sure you're having good dreams
Because she secretly fights off all of the demons you keep
Although she's broken it is you.
Her baby that makes her heart beat whole
And every time she hears your sweet laugh

Just like medicine it heals her soul
One tired mom is too exhausted to play
But she never stopped thinking of you and wondering if
you were OK
While watching the clock counting each minute and
second
That she had no choice but to spend away
One tired mom who God sent from above
She is in fact the first and only woman you'll ever love
No matter what, never be part
Unconditionally the only one that truly understands you
Fix you by putting you back together
All the hurt that you have held within your heart
One tired mom filled with so much rage
She will help you write an end to this chapter in your life
And flip it over to a new blank page
She will hold your hand and guide you through
The only one woman who sincerely cheers you on
As you embrace what she has taught you
And share with others as you take center stage.

CHAPTER 15
SELF-CENTERED

Constant lies
Unfaithful deeds
No understanding
But for their own needs
Words are solid
Hard as a stone
Spoken without thought
But you hurt me intentionally
Go ahead, kill me
Finish what you started
Completely breaking every bone
No trust and no loyalty
No compassion for me
Your accusations are wrong
They do not acknowledge any good or see
Blind to your surroundings
Believe in what you want
I don't hear anymore
I deserve happiness and love
My right, my value is one without war

SHE NEEDED THAT JOB

She needed a job
No longer be a slob
Just a reliable check holding her name
To gain independence and be no longer insane
Although she became sick of boredom,
And feeling totally lame
It was all in her head
So only herself could she blame
She needed a job
So she dressed up and did something new
She put on her heels and her makeup too
Then she gave her best
She took the shot
She applied for the job
That she so desperately did want.
She needed a job
Now she had one she loved
Helping people in masks and gloves
Working hard made her feel like a woman so complete
Achieving success gratefully
No chance to be a victim of defeat
She's definitely one-of-a-kind, simply unique
She makes friends with everyone she meets
And everyone listens and stops everything
As soon as she starts to speak

CHAPTER 17
WANNA KNOW ABOUT ME

Wanna know about me
Simply ask your questions
And I will answer honestly
I stay true to myself
With a heart full of devotion
Possessing no hesitation
To whomever is expressing my emotions
Wanna know about me
Please ask me these questions
I will always keep it real
My trust you must have
Or else my lips will stay sealed
I'm caught fighting life's battle
You can see my war scars
Still tryna heal and got no feel
Emotionally broken and unable to deal
Wanna know about me
They call me breezy because
I'm like a feather in the wind
Just going with the breeze
Nothing holds me back
Enjoying the surrounding trees
I fly freely and flow with ease
Yes, I am little and? So what?
Wanna know about me
I hate it when people tease
Don't judge me
I'm quick on my feet
I got secured credibility
To always keep my seat

Wanna know about me
I'm from the hood, imma boss
Not my friend? Too bad for you
That's your loss
Make me smile then watch to see
How easy it is that I am to please
I wish to travel one day and see the world
Exploring what exactly is located overseas.
Wanna know about me
I'm truly far from lame
Knowing my own importance
Surrounded by so much fame
Got my protection around me always
Playing life's crazy game
Psychotic stalkers know my name
Watching and defending me
Actions show they won't be tame
All these bees were in the trap
Pictures proved just to bring me to shame.

STEP DOWN

Fuck what you think
About me being so short
I wont step down
Even when I reached my last resort
Fuck what words you're saying
Just keep my name out of your mouth
This job is work, so stop fucking playing
Keep your asses busy
Down here in the south
All I ask for is a little respect
That's been damn well earned
But you obviously don't know about that.
Just take a step down now
Since apparently the tables have turned
With your fake asses full of jealousy
Cause you see here a real boss
Just because you see me smile
Doesn't mean you or I are dumb
So stop with the questions
Got me feeling like I'm on trial
Just mind your own business
And take yourself some kind of pill
Do your damn job so you can pay your own bills
Cause I will never step down from being me
And that's real so take a deep breath in and just chill
Fuck this fast food and all it stands for
This crap should be thrown out the door
Handed straight to the poor
Why must people have to be so mean
Just a bunch of damn bullies

Just looking to make a big scene
I wish people were more like me
With such a big heart
That I wear on my sleeve
Just wanting to help those being bullied
Those in need should finally be set free

CHAPTER 19
JUST STAY

You make me laugh
When I want more than to cry
You allow me to live
When I want to die
You make me smile
When you see me, you frown
You turn my whole world
Upside down and inside out
You believe in me
When no one else does
You are my now, my is, and ever was
I need you more than you can believe
I love you more than
You could ever conceive
I think of you every night and every day
And I hope my life with you
Will you please forever stay
From this moment to this very day
We will do things only in your way.

CHAPTER 20
BONDED LOVE

Soon everything will simply fall into place
It's all in patience until we have our own place
A guaranteed promise you will soon plainly see
The truth behind our own insecurities
A simple solution that will set us both free
I may be young, beautiful, and gifted
Some might even say that I'm smart
No matter just know you're the only one
Who holds the key to my whole heart
There may be millions of choices out there
To choose from but my choice is still you
Whatever in fact makes you happy my love
Just tell me what it is that I need to do
You are my hero, my rock, my ride or die
My amazing addiction, a new kind of high
I know I've been hard to deal with lately
You might even say I'm a royal pain in your ass
Maybe I'm driving you insane but I don't mean to horas
Just have a little faith and patience with these hormones
Of mine cause they too shall pass
I'm sorry for not being myself and not giving you my all
I'm so filled with hurt that has yet to have the time to
entirely heal
I fear you not catching me each time I fall
Or understanding and listening to me when I say how
I feel
Help me find a solution to a questionable problem
Differentiating what love we have is such a big deal
I have realized the truth beyond our reality

What we have is so special to get to hold
One strong bonded love woven tightly together as one
My one promise is to never fold
Happily together forever while growing old

CHAPTER 21
TRUE MAGIC

After all these years
of her growing life
She can't believe she is finally engaged
She had finally found the one and powerful
Who holds the key to unlock her cage
Who opened the doors to her happiness
And helped her to turn over a new page
Her first real taste of freedom
Her eyes open to see the world in a whole new
Like a butterfly her wings had finally opened
Revealing one's true beauty no one could deny
What once was a dream
It is now starting to come true
Both are so deeply in love
Together forever as one
Life itself has made them turn immortal
And time pauses for an instant
As they both stare deep into each others eyes
While joining together hand in hand
They kiss and like magic their bodies begin to float
Hovering slowly off the ground and
Heading up towards the sky
Having not ever known the power of love
Being in love, finding your soulmate without knowing
Until the first kiss, that is what magic does to make
you fly

CHAPTER 22

BUILDING RAGE

She wasn't supposed to even be home
But she slouched in her recliner
In her dark living room all alone
On her table lay a big bag of weed
And in her hands, they were gripped tightly
There was a liquor bottle of Patron.
Which she could drink consistently.
And was known to always smoke
She could smoke a full blunt within one toke
However, when she drink
She couldn't find the will to stop
She continued to drink it all
Down to the very last drop
But when darkness falls she refuses to sleep
Scared of losing the precious soul that she keeps
Only slumbering in the day of light
Avoiding demons in the shadows that hide
Who are just waiting for her soul to fight
Trying to take her most precious memories
Like a thief in the night
The deed is done now
She has reached her level
So fucked up, she became a rebel
So full of depression and just fed up
Exhausted from being abused
So ready for a change from the drugs she once used
Caught up in emotions overflowing with so much
negative rage
So mad at the world regardless of age
This is how she is and who she has become

Tired of being stepped on continuously
People seem to think she's dumb
She hides in the darkness yet still preys
Only for the light of day to come
To cleanse away her bad revengeful rage
She's ready for a new and happy beginning
A whole new life is now turning on a new page.

CHAPTER 23
BLACK BANNED ANGEL

She hides in her cave
But she never came out
All alone in society
Scared they might learn what she's about
Possessing a secret that
Creates a change in many lives
A powerful and magical one
That will leave you covered in hives
She's special indeed at first
And from the very start
One beauty Devine
Guaranteed to break a man's heart
Taking all her pain and
Concealing it, and locking it away
Saving it for the future
Allowing it to become useful one day
Once an angel, until losing her wings
Because of her refusal to obey
What they called the great kings
Which who banned her from heaven
Doomed for all eternity on earth
Making one choice and not considering
In fact just what she was worth
Her smile is so bright
Her long curly red hair
Shines beautifully with her eyes so big and blue
But with her mission failed
She continued to stay true
Granting others their wishes
Showing them what's real
Till the day she got caught
Then the king's knew she was in fact a big deal.

CHAPTER 24

MOTIVATIONAL SPEECH

Open your beautiful eyes
Keep positive thoughts of your future
Throw back your bedroom blinds
And let the bright sun shine in
Keep your beautiful smile glowing
And you can be sure to win
Always show your true colors
No matter where you have been
Though life as we know it
Is continuously overflowing with sin
Stay true to yourself
Keep journeying towards the bright light
Learn to accept reality.
And never stop your fight
Never give up on your true purpose
You serve in this life itself
Believe it or not you'll end up in great wealth
Your luck is in fact changing
You will soon plainly see
Keep an eye on the ball
Be who you are intended to be
As time passes by your eyes will open
Allowing you to see the truth in all reality
That is the key to releasing you
That will finally set you free

CHAPTER 25
TALKING SHIT

All he does is constantly talk shit
I can't stand his voice
Not the least little bit
He thinks he's a boss talking shit
But in reality, he's just a little bitch
Running his mouth on people talking shit
So we know he's a snitch
He's messing with innocent lives and talking shit
Busting heads and taking names
Destroying people with his fucked up head games
Continuously bullying people, both left and right
Running his mouth, talking shit
Just trying to start a fight
Constantly showing his disrespect
Gonna one day get himself shot
Prancing around like a badass thinking he's hot
He had a choice but refused to pick
To show respect and have a life with me or continue
being a bum
Making his money while sucking dick
Praying for a mute button, so hell quit talking shit
This man needs the shit beat out of him
Including his last drop of shit talking spit
The psychic sees his future which shows nothing but bad
His stealing, lying and cheating are sad all
That talking shit, he needs to learn to shut his mouth
Or soon he will find out all that I'm about
He needs to quit his current ways of talking shit
Or he will be sure to blaze in hell
For the rest of his days

Only time will tell until he eats a barrel
For talking shit you're gonna end up being killed
That will be the last day of him talking shit. His lips will
finally stay sealed.
I won't know anything, because I'll let Karma pay
what's due.

CHAPTER 26
PERFECT ADVISE

Get your shit right
Or we can fist fight
Give it your all
No matter what falls
Learn to forget your past
Cause the future will forever last
Keep your happy memories
And never retire your smile
Please kick off your shoes
And just stay for a while
Continue holding on tightly
To your only piece of good luck
Cause only you have the power
To prevent getting fucked
Love life today but
Always look forward to tomorrow
Learn how to say no to letting everyone borrow
Continue doing good deeds
Always helping a random stranger out
Remember where you came from
Without any doubt,
Who you are inside down here in the south
No matter what you see tonight
Just keep drinking sweet tea and
Try to watch your mouth.

CHAPTER 27

THE DEMON INSIDE

. . .

As I walk through this life
I carry baggage gained throughout the years
Continuously wearing out my backbone
Creating a long river
Made completely out of shredded tears
The pain is not simple
Nor easy to explain
With a terrible ache in my heart
That makes me wish more for rain
It hurts so badly, it's driving me insane
Driving my anguish, building more darkness
Which I've kept buried deep inside
A creation of spirit is so powerful
It refuses to run away and hide
Only revealing itself
When negativity lingers around
Gaining power while growing stronger
Just enough to stand its ground
When someone makes me angry
It's like they flip a switch
And I began shaking so bad
The demons took over my body completely
You can see it within my eyes
Nothing left but being so sad.
Getting pleasure from my pain
Hurting anyone who gets in its path
My open wounds need a chance to heal
While I feel my emotional wrath

CHAPTER 28

FAKE PEOPLE

Fake people, fake worlds and fake lives
We love to hate but hate to love
Fluttering in and out
Like the wings of a dove
Lesson learned: We made a deal
Stop the fake ass shit
And start being real
Let's live our lives without regrets
And do our damnedest not
To get lost in big debt
We are all only human
As you can plainly tell
If we don't quit our ways
Well, you'll be sure to end up in hell
Fucking fake people
Let's be real adults here
Let's quit our stupid fights
Let's grow the hell up
And finally make the shit right
I'm tired of fame.
Cause it's really getting lame
Your head games will not tame me
Or ever knock me down
Cause I choose to be happy
When you are around
Let's rock this life and
Let's make it our bitch
Fuck those fake asses
Cause all they do is snitch
Then run away like a bitch

Running their mouths at 100mph
With their fake ass shit
Gonna keep it up
And wound up in a ditch
Fucking fake people.

CHAPTER 29
AN EXPIRED RELATIONSHIP

The rumors are true
That in fact I have changed
Cause everything about me is different
And now completely rearranged
I stand in fear now
After almost losing my life
Became a complete failure
of being a good wife
I expect to receive nothing
But your disrespect knows I once
Cared too much when no one else did
You made me feel neglect
With the deepest sadness
Leaving my heart so hurt
One complete and total failure
For us two to make amends
I tried all I could to share and
Have happiness and fun with you again
Even though today you stand alone
While I continue to be bitter, I stand strong
So an apology would be nice
Just admit it once that you were wrong
Even though nothing is left of us or
Our foundation we once stood on
You have constantly failed me
Over and over again
Your choice of words is hard as stone
Hit me with each and every one
Breaking every single bone
There's nothing you can say

That will forever change our past
Its simply over, it's done with
Our love has hit its expiration
Miserably, it failed to last
I tried to communicate with you
I tried to make complete amends
You laughed in my face
Denying all that I am worth
Directly in front of your so-called friends
So all of a sudden you want to talk
Knowing they were over and now I had chosen someone
else
Because you can't stand to see me happy
Overflowing with love and being in complete good health
I refuse to be in misery because of you
I give a fuck if you care
Friends are like grass. You can kiss my ass
Your life that you live is unfair
I'm getting married and it's too late
We have a family on the way
He takes care of me and understands me
Always listen to every word that I say
Love me unconditionally each and every day
Sincere goodbyes, I have no time
To hear your lies, no time
For questioning how or why
Just be a man and leave it the hell alone
What's done is done so
You can take your ass back home
You can get a life and go to church
The perfect place to find
Your next victimized wife

CHAPTER 30
MAKE-UP NOTE

Millions of thoughts are processed
Over and over in my mind
All that I want to say to you
Comes out blended together and all combined
All at once at the same exact time
So let me stop for a second
Let me press rewind
Please give me a chance to explain
Exactly how you make me feel
Let me show you how much I love you
Let me prove to you that I'm real
I'm sincerely trying to make you happy
Myself as well still having fun
Enjoying life and doing my best
Becoming one big family
Bending over backwards for you
Complete tasks without question
Hope one day you will make me your wife
Here lately it seems that no matter what I do
You always stay upset or sad
It kills me to see you like that
More challenging to achieve happiness
Face the facts it's getting bad
I completely understand that
Its a negative environment
Yet I'm confused why you refuse to leave
I just wish I had the answers to your questions
The key to unlocking positivity
What is sure to set your soul free
I want you so badly

And not just one piece
Sincerely all over you instead
With an understanding of who I am
And what I will in fact become
Sharing more moments of intimacy
At least attempt to change it up
I want to experiment and try new things
Not have to beg to give me some of you
After denials from you at times
So frustrated with you
Only wanting us both to be one

CHAPTER 31

THE CHOSEN PATH TO NOTHING

No matter what I do or say
I scream, I holler, I cry or I pray
Nothing ever seems to help
And life keeps getting in my way
I tried my best but nothing works
See within the shadows, the demons lark
Playing games and laughing while mocking me
And the choices I made please help me out
Please understand I'm faked by failure
I need to succeed, my sanity grows strongly
At stake, i plead, i beg, i fall to my knees
Asking God why. No solution is the answer
My actions have become just wasted time
Success surrounds my whole world
My happiness quickly just passes by
I found a job but no way to work
With no way to get there
I'm steadily going bazurk
I finally found a car but have no money to buy
Not enough trade points to even fly
I can't go to college
Cause I do better online
I'm hopeless, a burden altogether defined.
My life sucks, I just need to make big bucks
My car needs to sell before I start raising hell
Or do something stupid and end up in jail
Then officially fail with no help to lead me
No sign of a trial, no prayers answered.
Stuck behind bars overnight
No luck in this hell hole

No way of making bail
I'm losing everything and I must do something fast
Before my forever sail away far
And there goes my love
I thought I would always last
Now alone, no lover and no car
No job and no phone
Homeless, no shelter, I grow cold
Nothing to talk about besides war scars
Taking from strangers after getting drunk here at the bar
Drunk karaoke singer becomes a true star.

MY VOWS TO YOU

Throughout the years
You have watched me beautifully grow
And slowly fall apart
You wiped away my tears
You learn by listening
Understanding me when no one else did
From the start you made me laugh
When I wanted more than to cry
Made me live when I wanted more than to die
Together we made our friendship solid
Built to last through the good and the
Bad times have flown by so fast
So distant for a year
But yet still so close
A relationship ended when I got badly hurt and almost died
You heard what happened
And immediately home to me you flied
I was broken completely
My heart had turned to stone
You knew of my fears and kept me
Close your arms
Reassuring me that I was not alone
You gave me security, compassion and love without end
So thank you for showing me
How to love again
You have mended my heart together
Carefully with each and every tare
Patiently waiting for me so now
I have a white dress for you that I will wear

I have seen your flaws both good and bad
I love you and your smile
You are the best I have ever had
I promise to accept you for all that you are
To be truly yours and only yours forever
Always follow you no matter how far

CHAPTER 33
EX DREAMS AND KISSES

Late night terror
Morning dreams
Consumed with fear,
From my silent screams
Realizing what is
It is not what it seems
These are my thoughts.
of a soulless being
Shivering, shaking, cold sweats at night
Fantasy grows stronger
of taking your site
Condemning you forever
To a permanent night
They slice your throat and try
Cutting your wrists
But as for your jugulars
He will certainly miss
Never forget your lips
of our very first kiss.

CHAPTER 34
BROKEN DOWN

Stranded in a town that she's never been
Her car broke down on a hot day of 110
No station was close by that the girl could attend
No cell phone reception
So no calls or texts would successfully be sent.
But she kept moving forward
While keeping her smile
From trying to unbend
Nothing could destroy her
Or ruin her good day
Knowing in fact she wasn't alone
She had to watch her every word
Her mouth would try to say
Enjoying the presence
of her very best friend
Her heart and soul
The air that she breathes
Forever in love with a pleasurable tease
Together they were in fact unstoppable
And motivated completely
Just two hard working bumble bees
They walked along the way
Till they both hit their knees
They begin to stop and pray for a miracle
To finally come true
As they begin to gain reception
To call a tow truck big and blue
Sweat pours down on their flesh
Which was burned by the sun's heat

Then waiting around begins to suck
Not even caring about the cost
Just want the broken down car to get fixed
And me and my friend finally getting un-stuck

CHAPTER 35

RAIN O RAIN

Rain o rain please calm my pain
Rain o rain you can drive me insane
Rain o rain your the first to take the blame
The rain floods the streets with a river
Cleansing my whole body
Replenishing each and every vain
A unique and beautiful disaster
In its own kind of way
Holding everyone inside just for today
No success today when the rain won't go away
Rain o rain please let me explain
Just why is it that you
Continue to still remain
Feeding my beautiful garden in such vain
You make my plants start growing
You bless it with beautiful colors
River rain water pouring
Rain o rain you will never know
Just how stupid I felt
Pushing you so hard to go
But you cleaned the air of all my past
Leaving for a new season that's bound to last

CHAPTER 36
FALLING TEARS

There's a story behind your falling tears
That truly expresses your emotion
It's hidden deep within your fears
Getting tired of fixing your mascara smears
Never able to grasp just who you are
With so much negativity that surrounds you
Voices constantly whispering nonsense
Into your precious ears
Stupid accusations that
Your friend continues to hear
That make your eyes create falling tears
You turn up the bottle of alcohol
To simply numb your pain
Dare you dream to die
Just let the poisonous juice
Flow throughout your veins
Falling tears keep flowing
Erasing bad memories
From your soul and brain
To love someone, then lose them
When they were in fact your whole world
It's the falling tears that
Are the keys to driving
A person completely insane

A BETTER ME

There's nothing I can say or tell myself
To simply try to change my mind
The person that I used to be
Is gone now and unable to find
Along with the smile that once existed
Has twisted now into a different kind
The past is done now so don't press rewind
Left with only good memories and thoughts
That begin replaying themselves over and over
within my own psychotic mind
What I once fought for I now have come to realize
It was not my war and not my fight
But to keep my faith and move forward
Becoming a better me is now my right
A sacrifice for victory to never loosing sight
What the future holds for me
And holds for my complete success
Without question this is my quest
Out with the old and in with the new
I'm rediscovering myself and finding the
Happiness that I know I deserve too.

CHAPTER 38
MEMORIES

Memories remain
Without any way to gain
What was lost
Now it is found
Living inside of you
Completely safe and sound
Keeping secrets
From all around
Inside your heart
Staying home bound
A love so close
Truly defined as
A complex overdose
Right from the start
We were never meant to be apart
Leaving our mark
Under every tree
But I never got
The chance with you
To venture out
And explore the sea
Memories are full of pain
Can you set me free and
Bring back that smile
Making me miss who I used to be

CHAPTER 39
SOMETHING

There's something in the water
Maybe even in the air
People are acting all crazy
Treating me so unfair
I tried to kill them with kindness
But now I'm pulling out my hair
So tired of something
That's something that's everywhere
within my house and
Out here in these streets
within my own car
Or down on my feet
Something peculiar about that
Just won't ever go away
It makes me miserable
Breaking me down every day.
Something that stays in my mind
Seems so important
But I'm unable to find
That something was put on pause
Unable to press rewind
Just something that's something.
Which can never be left behind

CHAPTER 40
EMOTIONAL STRUGGLE

She let herself go just to care for everyone else
She went out of her way for others all the time
Then she forgot her own worth and ended up losing
herself
And endured the pain of her overall health
She tried her damnedest to wind up good wealth
But nothing could save her from an emotional mess.
All the bad thoughts overcame her mind causing stress
Forming a twisting hurricane that
Danced in her head and was complete total chaos
That will soon kill her dead
She endured a rough life
And every day becomes an emotional struggle
No one to talk to
And no one to share cuddles
She smiles from the outside
Yet still crying from deep within
Only karma is left as her comfort
She eventually learned how to be a friend
No one else understands her
Without judging where she has been
Everyone around seems completely fake
So she stays hidden in her kitchen
Where she continues to bake
A type of therapy that takes the cake
Just a struggle within her emotions
Grieving the memories she let go of
Like a sail boat out into the ocean.

CHAPTER 41
LOVE NOTE

There's never a day that passes
When I don't think of you
I'm always wondering where I went wrong
Or why I did the things I did.
You believe in me
When no one else did
You faced my fears and fought for me
While I cowered down behind you and hid
I shower myself in tears
Unable to face reality with my peers
So I drowned myself in drugs and beer
Which allowed me to hide from
What truly is and was my deepest fear?
When at my lowest you never departed
But instead, they gave me
All your love and support
Showed understanding
To the brokenhearted.
I tried everything to push you away
And deep down you know that
I need you to please stay
I never knew love until I met you
And after three years together
I still get butterflies too
I love the way you can still make me laugh
When I want more than to cry
The way you kiss and touch me is
When I refuse to ever say goodbye
Now that we have a son
Our life together has gotten messy

But we still find ways to have lots of fun
Still full of love and laughter
I couldn't imagine our lives any other way
I'm content with our happy ever after
I feel so honored that you chose me
I'm so glad to call you mine
It's us against the world as we know it
I will be your bonnie if you are my Clyde
Till death do us part love
Together we shall ride out this storm
Together we shall concur in the ocean tide.

CHAPTER 42
DEATH NOTE

My love my life
Always there for me
So forever I will be his wife
Ignore my cries of pain
Since I became broken
I'm no longer the same
Still trapped in the past
And somehow unable to grasp
What was, what is and
What will be becomes clear
Regardless of what
Exactly what you want to hear
I will present the truth to you
As I stand before you
And face my biggest fear
Trying my hardest to hold myself together
Fighting back with each and every tear
I since my death is coming soon
My body aches all over
On this night of a full moon
With such a unique design
Just like our love for one another
Definitely one of a special kind
When you found me, I was damaged
And the broken pieces of my heart
You accepted me for all of my flaws
Mending every tear that you didn't break
Showing me love was a risk you had to take.
For I knew my life was almost over
Becoming so sick of life's abuse

It was then that I vowed to get sober
On that day in my darkest hour
You found me at my lowest after losing all my power
It was then that I looked death in the face
But like a knight in shining armor
You were in fact my amazing grace
Love had no definition until the day I met you
Suicide had been reconsidered the day at the alter
When we exchanged vows and both said, "I do!"
God has blessed us without validation to describe
And was there answering every prayer to him we confide
My love my life my ride or die till the end
Us against the world as one
An unraveling tornado of events
A love story that's incomplete.
One prayer we never finished sending
The pandemic happened and
It seemed like everything was starting to fall apart
Staying strong beside me
Even with my whole world crumbling down
Because of our children we will be together forever and
always at heart
Never truly can we really part
Even when we both express a frown.
Our day starts turning upside down
We will always remember how we tried

CHAPTER 43

JESUS, I NEED YOU

Jesus, I need you
I'm steadily losing my mind
Constantly hearing voices
That does not seem very kind
I have tried to ignore them
Set back and try to rewind
But what these voices are saying
Makes me want to commit suicide.
Jesus, I need you
Help me to win this hard battle I face
To fight off demons
That still reside here in this place
Give me the strength to accept my convictions
And defeat this war against all my addictions
Jesus, I need you
Not just tomorrow but as well as today
I'm ready to put you first
Because it's all in your name Jesus
That only seems to quench my thirst
So I'm trusting you completely
I'm putting all of these burdens in your hands
This I pray to the miracle worker
My redeemer, my master and my savior
Let it be all in your will and
Make everything turn out okay
Jesus, I need you
Help me to stay focused
To be a better person than I was before
Allow me to understand and clearly see
Why that it is you

Closed that certain door
Jesus, I need you
I need you now more than ever before
I cry and beg for forgiveness
Till both of my eyes become sore
I'm here to accept my convictions
Admitting my soul and body need you Jesus
As I lay crunched up on the floor
Help me to conquer this emotional war
And free me from these chains made by my addictions
and forgive me of all of my prior convictions
Jesus, I need you.

CHAPTER 44
THE BUTTERFLY

Beautiful winged bugs
Each uniquely designed their own
So many colors and shapes combined
Displayed so brightly and truly defined
To be considered to be one of a kind
Butterflies are their name
And none are the same
They fly so free like I wish I could be
Never to be tamed, unforgettably named
When my day comes, I should die
Just stop and look up at the big blue sky
Begin your search for a beautiful butterfly
For there I will be smiling at you you'll see
Showing off my new colorful bright wings
I will land on your shoulder and wait for you
To see just what it is the heavens hold for me
I will soak up the sun and enjoy the breeze
I will listen to the birds' song that they sing
Just a reminder to never forget
How I made a difference in your life
While I was once alive
Become something bigger than just a memory trying to
survive
Cause the wings I've earned are those of a butterfly
So if you find yourself questioning just where I went
and why
After I die please do not cry
Just remember who I am when I visit you from heaven
Like a big beautiful butterfly.

CHAPTER 45
HUSTLE

So tired of not being productive
I feel like such a slob
Maybe I might feel better
Once I gain a dependable job
No more worrying about
How much money will I make?
Or trying to hustle
To put it all on one plate
The people I work with seem pretty nice
I just need to keep my opinions to myself
And remember not to give anyone advice
Ill tell them I'm here
To work and not socialize
Got to stay within my zone
As I'm unloading office supplies
Should I stay or should I go
Another job offers way more
It's a work from home position
So no gas will be needed
To get me out of the door
All I know to do is hustle and work
Work hard like I was trained to do
I will keep on praying for a blessing
Hope my job skills will
Makes quite an overall impression
I can hustle and get money
Using all I already know
I will make some jewelry
I will craft some art
I will bake all kinds of goods

From the bottom of my heart
I love to hustle and make it legit
No need to lie cheat or steal
And the best part of all
I don't break a sweat.
I will pick up the old furniture
And restore it to good as new
Ill take a dive into a dumpster
If it holds something of value
And I can get past the stench
I love fixing and creating something
setting on a park bench
They call me Mrs. Fix a lot
Cause I don't need a tool or a wrench
Then I'll buy me a booth
Down on the market
And there is where all
My crafts will set and park it
Guaranteed to stand out like
The clearance tags at Target.
And that's how you really hustle
Making money in today's society
While celebrating a year of sobriety.

CHAPTER 46
HARD TIMES

Hard times are here
And I cannot seem to focus
Just what I need to do
There's so much going on around me
I've become overwhelmed altogether
And caught up in my emotions too
Continuous thoughts replay like
A broken record within my mind
I'm left with the feeling
Something is missing and not knowing
What was lost scares me in knowing
Just what might I find?
Behind the shaded window blinds
Hard times are here
And even though I had quit drinking
Now might be the time
To pass me a damn beer
Cause no matter what
I try to do I'm a failure
And what makes it even worse is
Always being stuck living within fear
Hard times are here
There's no doubt about the reason.
Getting harder to keep my family safe
Regardless of all the screwed up seasons
I feel like I'm drowning
Since so long I've been staying afloat
Taxes just keep growing
More bills keep on coming in and flowing
Just wish I could take

A pause and stop time
Taking a break and resting my mind
Since nothing seems to break me free
The struggles and burdens of reality
Become attached to me
Finding what I need to reach success
Hard times are here because there's
No hustle in me left, I must confess
The rules that are legal without
Socializing or having to mingle
While pretending that you're single
In order to make money
With all your experienced wrinkles
Such beautiful eyes.
You possess displayed a twinkle
You cannot be trialed to see what it is that you never
reaped
Somehow it found my struggles and
Fears of a long and narrow dead-end street
No matter how much I run
From the bills, they still consume me
Always staying right between my feet
Hard times are here
There's no time for confession.
Unable to grasp a hold of my deep depression
As I seem to be winning,
Only because we are in a recession
I don't want to break my back
Worshiping the olé mighty dollar
I'd rather die worshiping my god
Even though this might sound crappy
I miss the feeling I had of being happy

When nothing like this even mattered
Even though I set with no money
With my family still by my side
Left me feeling loved and flattered
The happiest I have felt before is like a
Whole new world born without control
Complete a new set of morals
And release the energy
Left from within your very own soul

CHAPTER 47
WHY?

Why does life as we know it
Have to be so damn hard
Why does my struggle
Never seem to want to end
Why does the burning pain
Inside me ceases to vanish
Why don't my demons return
Back to hell and resend
Why do I constantly feel
My heart breaks into a million pieces
Inability to repair or mend
Why does life keep throwing me choices
When obviously I'm unable to choose
Why do drugs appear
Out of no ear like magic
When I reached the point
In my addiction, I finally gave in
Why does the devil find pleasure
In tormenting my life with abuse
I set here in prayer
Accepting my conviction while
Fighting back against the strong urge to use
Why does every storm we make it through
Just brings more sadness into my life
Tears build up in my eyes
Every time I hear bad news
Why is it so hard to stay positive?
The negative thoughts getting rebuked

www.ingramcontent.com/pod-product-compliance
Lightning Source LLC
Chambersburg PA
CBHW051127160726
47997CB00018B/810